"Dustin Benge provides us wi̲th̲ ̲a̲ ̲. . .a̲tion of all that is good about the local church. With ease of prose, Benge introduces us to the multicolored facets of what the church is and how she functions to grow us into the people of God. A marvelous read."

Derek W. H. Thomas, Senior Minister, First Presbyterian Church, Columbia, South Carolina; Teaching Fellow, Ligonier Ministries; Chancellor's Professor, Reformed Theological Seminary

"The true and faithful church is the beautiful bride of Christ. In the experience of reading this refreshing treatment, all who love the church will rejoice in the realization of her beauty. Many people are concerned about how the world views the church. The world will never have the right perspective until the church itself sees her beauty. Surely this is what the apostle Paul meant when he said in 2 Corinthians 11:2 that he desired to present the church as a chaste virgin to Christ. This book is a much-needed gift to the people of God."

John MacArthur, Pastor, Grace Community Church, Sun Valley, California; Chancellor, The Master's University and Seminary

"This is a rich reflection upon the nature of the church. Benge rightly shows us the way the church is viewed from heaven and from the eschaton. If we could only grasp the glorious beauty of the church in the light of these two perspectives, the negativity that too often crosses our lips and permeates our minds about the triune God's beloved would be replaced with wonder and awe. Warmly recommended."

Michael A. G. Haykin, Chair and Professor of Church History, The Southern Baptist Theological Seminary

"A little more than a decade ago I said I'd never seen such a profound unity in the church. What has happened? Leadership failures, unresolved conflicts, high-profile apostasies, political division, social upheaval, a global pandemic, theological controversy, and more. Is greater church unity possible again? Of course it is, but any movement toward unity must be dependent on the Holy Spirit and based on God's truth. May the Lord use this book, in which Dustin Benge faithfully sets forth the glories of God's truth about the church, to rebuild our unity."

Donald S. Whitney, Professor of Biblical Spirituality and Associate Dean, The Southern Baptist Theological Seminary

"Do you consider the church to be lovely? Jesus does. He looks at his blood-bought bride with deep delight and desires that we do the same. In *Why Should We Love the Local Church?* Dustin Benge introduces us afresh to the church in a way that rekindles affection and renews commitment. Many books tell us about the church, but few help us love the church. This important work refreshes the soul and inspires worship."

Garrett Kell, Lead Pastor, Del Ray Baptist Church, Alexandria, Virginia

"Beholding the true beauty of the church can often be a challenge because many times she is torn asunder by various scandals and divisions. Dustin Benge nevertheless calls us to view the church from the divine perspective as the chosen bride of Christ. Only through this corrective lens can we recognize how precious she is in the sight of our triune God. May God give us eyes to see her radiant glory as she is clothed with the glistening garments of Christ."

Steven J. Lawson, President, OnePassion Ministries; Professor of Preaching, The Master's Seminary; Teaching Fellow, Ligonier Ministries

WHY SHOULD WE LOVE
THE LOCAL CHURCH?

Union

A book series edited by Michael Reeves

Rejoice and Tremble: The Surprising Good News of the Fear of the Lord, Michael Reeves (2021)

What Does It Mean to Fear the Lord?, Michael Reeves (2021, concise version of *Rejoice and Tremble*)

Deeper: Real Change for Real Sinners, Dane C. Ortlund (2021)

How Does God Change Us?, Dane C. Ortlund (2021, concise version of *Deeper*)

The Loveliest Place: The Beauty and Glory of the Church, Dustin Benge (2022)

Why Should We Love the Local Church?, Dustin Benge (2022, concise version of *The Loveliest Place*)

WHY SHOULD WE LOVE THE LOCAL CHURCH?

DUSTIN BENGE

CROSSWAY®

WHEATON, ILLINOIS

Why Should We Love the Local Church?

Copyright © 2022 by Dustin Benge

Published by Crossway
    1300 Crescent Street
    Wheaton, Illinois 60187

Cover design: Jordan Singer

Cover image: "New England Scenery" (1839) by Thomas Cole (Wikimedia commons)

First printing 2022

Printed in the United States of America

Scripture quotations are from the ESV® Bible (The Holy Bible, English Standard Version®), copyright © 2001 by Crossway, a publishing ministry of Good News Publishers. Used by permission. All rights reserved.

All emphases in Scripture quotations have been added by the author.

Trade paperback ISBN: 978-1-4335-7498-6
ePub ISBN: 978-1-4335-7501-3
PDF ISBN: 978-1-4335-7499-3
Mobipocket ISBN: 978-1-4335-7500-6

Library of Congress Cataloging-in-Publication Data

Names: Benge, Dustin W., author.
Title: Why should we love the local church? / Dustin Benge.
Other titles: Loveliest place
Description: Wheaton, Illinois : Crossway, 2022. | Series: Union | Includes bibliographical references and index.
Identifiers: LCCN 2021023824 (print) | LCCN 2021023825 (ebook) | ISBN 9781433574986 (trade paperback) | ISBN 9781433574993 (pdf) | ISBN 9781433575006 (mobipocket) | ISBN 9781433575013 (epub)
Subjects: LCSH: Church.
Classification: LCC BV600.3 .B46252 2022 (print) | LCC BV600.3 (ebook) | DDC 262.001/7—dc23
LC record available at https://lccn.loc.gov/2021023824
LC ebook record available at https://lccn.loc.gov/2021023825

Crossway is a publishing ministry of Good News Publishers.

VP			31	30	29	28	27	26	25	24	23	22
15	14	13	12	11	10	9	8	7	6	5	4	3	2	1

To Nate Pickowicz,
my friend, brother,
and co-laborer in the gospel

Contents

Series Preface

OUR INNER CONVICTIONS and values shape our lives and our ministries. And at Union—the cooperative ministries of Union School of Theology, Union Publishing, Union Research, and Union Mission (visit www.theolo.gy)—we long to grow and support men and women who will delight in God, grow in Christ, serve the church, and bless the world. This Union series of books is an attempt to express and share those values.

They are values that flow from the beauty and grace of God. The living God is so glorious and kind, he cannot be known without being adored. Those who truly know him will love him, and without that heartfelt delight in God, we are nothing but hollow hypocrites. That adoration of God necessarily works itself out in a desire to grow in Christlikeness. It also fuels a love for Christ's precious bride, the church, and a desire humbly to serve—rather than use—her. And, lastly, loving God brings us to share his concerns, especially to see his life-giving glory fill the earth.

Each exploration of a subject in the Union series will appear in two versions: a full volume and a concise one. The concise treatments, such as this one, are like shorter guided tours: they stick to the main streets and move on fast. You may find, at the end of this little book, that you have questions or want to explore some more: in that case, the fuller volume will take you further up and further in.

My hope and prayer is that these books will bless you and your church as you develop a deeper delight in God that over-flows in joyful integrity, humility, Christlikeness, love for the church, and a passion to make disciples of all nations.

Michael Reeves
SERIES EDITOR

Introduction

WE ALL HAVE SPECIAL PLACES we visit, either in person or in memory. For me, one of those treasured places is the farm of my grandparents. Running through freshly plowed fields, climbing majestic oaks, and sitting at the table of my grandmother's cooking—there's no place I would rather be. This place evokes a sense of joy, comfort, and home.

When we think of the church, does it arouse similar deep affection? Can we say the church is one of those unique places that conjures a sincere sense of longing, delight, and home?

It's all too easy to allow our warmth toward the church to slip away, as we grow cold and apathetic. Honestly, the church can often be a difficult place to think of as *lovely*. However, when we shift our perspective from our puny self-interest, which often fuels our disgruntlement toward the church, she not only becomes precious to us but also becomes a treasure of eternal joy, beauty, and glory.

This book is about the loveliness, beauty, and glory of the church. It's for all those who sometimes struggle to see those qualities in her. If you tirelessly serve within her ministries while dismayed by her apparent failures, or have rare, unsustainable glimpses of her beauty, this book is for you. The singular goal is to awaken your affections. Not affections for form, methodology, structure, organization, or programs, but affections for *who* she is and *why* she exists.

There is no more robust and doxological foundation upon which we can build a definition of the church than the eternal work of the Father, Son, and Holy Spirit. In the words of eighteenth-century New England pastor-theologian Jonathan Edwards, the whole world was created so that "the eternal Son of God might obtain a spouse."[1] The church is not a Trinitarian afterthought in response to man's fall in the garden—quite the contrary. The church is the focused domain where all God's presence, promises, and purposes are unveiled and eternally realized.

The church's beauty and loveliness are most vividly portrayed in the brilliant metaphor of her as the "bride of Christ." In his instructions to husbands regarding the love they should have for their wives, the apostle Paul writes, "Love your wives, as Christ loved the church and gave himself up for her" (Eph. 5:25). This stunning bride is arrayed in snow-white garments washed in the redeeming blood of Christ (Rev. 7:14), and beholding her beauty, a vast multitude cries out,

> The marriage of the Lamb has come,
>> and his Bride has made herself ready. (Rev. 19:7)

God gives the church to Christ as his bride, Edwards says, "so that the mutual joys between this bride and bridegroom are the end of the creation."[2]

As the creation of God, the church is a means through which the Father delights in Christ as the object of his eternal love and divine happiness. The church's life is beautifully framed by her position as the reward to Christ for his suffering on the cross, thus making Christ a worthy groom for his bride. This glorious union between Christ and his church will never be severed. The two, joined together by God, are eternally satisfied in one another as they bask in the glory, majesty, and holiness of God.

This book has one aim: to set before you a thoroughly biblical portrait of the church that derives its life from the sweet fellowship of the Father, Son, and Spirit, creating a community of love, worship, fellowship, and mission, all animated by the gospel and empowered by the word of God.

By beholding such radiant beauty and loveliness, may we lift our collective and worshipful cry, "Indeed, the church is the loveliest place on earth."

You Are Beautiful

Behold, you are beautiful, my love;
behold, you are beautiful.
SONG OF SOLOMON 1:15

THE CHURCH HAS PLAYED a central role in many of our lives. She has nurtured in times of grief, shepherded in valleys of despair, and instructed in seasons of growth.

We love her people. We love her ministries. We love her worship. We love her teaching. We love her comfort.

Do we love her?

Admired by Christ

Reflecting on Song of Solomon 1:15, John Gill, an eighteenth-century English Baptist pastor, wrote, "These are the words of

Christ, commending the beauty of the church, expressing his great affection for her, and his high esteem of her; of her fairness and beauty."[1] Gill interprets Song of Solomon as an intense allegorical portrayal of the love, union, and communion that exists between Jesus Christ and his bride, the church. The bridegroom fixes his eternal attention upon the bride and identifies her as "beautiful."

What must it be like to be admired by the sinless Son of God? Rather than admire her, we imagine he would identify her failures, her shortcomings, and the loathsome sin that so often spoils her garments.

The church is beautiful because the lens through which Christ regards her is his cross—the focal point of blood, righteousness, forgiveness, union, justification, regeneration, and grace. Ultimately, the cross of the Lord Jesus Christ makes her beautiful. It is his sacrificial, substitutionary, sinless blood that washes her garments as white as snow. The cross of Christ makes her beautiful not only inwardly by justification but also outwardly through sanctification. From giving second birth to final glory, the righteousness of Christ creates a beautiful bride.

Reflected Beauty

The supreme expression of God's beauty is his Son, Jesus Christ, who himself is the image and radiance of his Father. Paul affirms Jesus as "the image of God" (2 Cor. 4:4). That is, to see Jesus is to see God, to hear Jesus is to hear God, to know Jesus is to know God. In Colossians 1:15, Paul classifies Jesus as "the image of the invisible God." As glory is a defining characteristic of God's nature, the beauty that shines forth from God also shines forth from Jesus, for Jesus is the visible incarnation of God's radiant glory.

To express God's infinite love for Christ, God gives him a spouse, the church. The church is a gift from God to his Son "so that," according to Jonathan Edwards, "the mutual joys between this bride and bridegroom are the end of creation."[2] Therefore, as the Son is a reflection of his Father, the church, as his eternal bride, is a reflection of the Son.

When Christ lovingly looks upon his bride and exclaims that she is "beautiful," he beholds the reflection of the everlasting glory and infinite love of his Father, who is the primary fountain from which all true beauty flows.

The church is beautiful because God is beautiful.

The Bride's Affection

Not only does Christ lavish his affection upon the church as the object of his joyful love, but the church also reveres her bridegroom with the same unshakable devotion. She describes him as "distinguished among ten thousand" (Song 5:10), having "lips

. . . dripping liquid myrrh" (v. 13), "arms . . . set with jewels" (v. 14), "legs . . . set on bases of gold" (v. 15), and "altogether desirable" (v. 16).

Of all who might arrest her attention, Jesus Christ is better than all the rest because he has purchased the church with his blood (Acts 20:28). Christ is beautiful to the church because he rescued her from her enemies and set her in heavenly places (Eph. 2:6). Christ is beautiful to the church because he freely offered his life as payment for a debt she owed (John 10:11). Christ is beautiful to the church because he satisfied God's wrath against her sin and victoriously conquered death (Rom. 3:24–25). Christ is her Savior. Christ is her Redeemer. Christ is her beauty.

2

The Household of God

I will be glory in her midst.

ZECHARIAH 2:5

GOD RESIDES EXPLICITLY in a distinctive and familial way among his people. God dwells in heaven in the sense that his glory, majesty, and holiness are on display there in particular richness. Yet he also assures his people that he will "be glory in [their] midst" (Zech. 2:5).

Moved by his inexhaustible love for the church before the foundation of the world, God resides in her midst with "every spiritual blessing in the heavenly places" (Eph. 1:3), so that even now those who are part of his family on earth are "seated . . . with him in the heavenly places in Christ Jesus" (Eph. 2:6).

God's Family

Defining the church in institutional terms is futile, for the church belongs exclusively to God. In 1 Timothy 3:15, Paul offers instructions in godliness so that we may know how "to behave in the *household of God*, which is the church of the living God." The word "household" elicits a metaphor not of a building or structure but of a family—those within the same house.

We are brothers and sisters to Christ through our second birth into his family (John 1:12–13). By nature, we are born in sin, wholly separated from God, but in Christ, we are adopted into God's family. Reading the New Testament is like looking through a family picture album or hearing the family history recited by a grandparent. The church is God's household and our family.

Defining Home

The church is defined by many words and phrases that identify her as being of heavenly origin. The English word *church* originates from the Greek term for those who belong to the Lord. This word derives from a title given to God as the sovereign Master over a people. The church is, therefore, God's special possession over which he resides as Master.

The church is most regularly associated with the Greek word *ekklēsia*, a term meaning "those who are called out" or "an assembly of the people." The church is uniquely those who have been called out of sinful darkness by God the Father through salvation in Jesus Christ, are now sealed by the Holy Spirit, and now belong to the Lord. The church thus finds her origin, beauty, and perfection in the triune God.

The Assembly of Mount Zion

Throughout his voluminous works, John Owen, a seventeenth-century Puritan theologian, offers a vivid image and description of the church. In his 1645 *Greater Catechism* he writes, "The whole company of God's elect, called of God, by the Word and Spirit, out of their natural condition, to the dignity of his children, and united unto Christ their head, by faith, in the bond of the Spirit."[1] Consistent with Paul's detailed description of those who are the church in Ephesians 1, Owen is careful to characterize the church as a Trinitarian and heavenly family made up of those whom God elects, calls, and unites to Christ through his lavish grace.

By definition, the church is constituted in a particular form. Various characteristics mark her: celebration of worship, preaching of the gospel, making disciples, the exercise of discipline, mutual edification, and the work of evangelism.[2] The church is best defined by both universal and local terminology. Theologians sometimes refer to these two categories as "invisible" and "visible." The invisible church is composed of believers worldwide, who have been elected, called, and regenerated. The visible church is those redeemed believers within a local congregation.

God's Home, Forever

Our one hope is the constant abiding presence of God—forever—which assures the church that God has not forsaken, nor will he ever forsake, his home. He will never love the church any less than he always has. He will never divorce the church. He will never go searching for a more attractive family. He will never move out or move away. The cascade of his love to her will never dissolve, for it runs from eternity past to eternity future.

God doesn't begrudgingly give himself to the church. He doesn't bemoan the home he has made among us. He doesn't regret pursuing us with his everlasting love. God delights to make the church his household and makes her beautiful by his presence among her.

3

Our Father and Friend

O LORD, you are our Father;
  we are the clay, and you are the potter;
  we are all the work of your hand.

ISAIAH 64:8

TO DEFINE THE CHURCH as a mere earthly institution or some entrepreneur's vision would be to miss completely who the church is in God's eternal mind and heart. The church's beauty comes into indefectible focus only when we peer through the lens of God's relationship to her. Anything less is choosing to play in mud puddles while refusing the vastness of the ocean.

Our Father

In Matthew 6, the disciples request that Jesus teach them how to pray. Jesus offers them something entirely unexpected to their old covenant way of thinking. He constructs a short prayer that serves as a pattern for all our conversations with God. While the prayer contains all the elements one might expect, Jesus addresses God using a personal name somewhat foreign to the Old Testament theological mind.

Under the old covenant, the children of God approached him in fear and trembling through the ritualism of priesthood and sacrifice. To enter his holy presence, the Israelites were required to meet with God through the tablernacle and temple. Though God was as much of a Father to believers in the Old Testament as he is in the New, Jesus brings God eternally close to the heart of the believer and invites us to bypass the priests, animal sacrifices, veils, and temples by offering us a vividly affectionate relationship with the sovereign of the universe: "Our Father in heaven" (Matt. 6:9).

God is the Father to his children in a way he is not to anyone else. He isn't only *a* Father or *the* Father, but he is *our* Father. He uniquely loves his church. The love of the Father always precedes our love toward him (1 John 4:19).

What does it mean for the church to call God "our Father"?

First, it's the end of self-exaltation. To confess that God is our Father is to acknowledge that we are helpless creatures and cannot rescue ourselves, for we need a Father who watches over us to save, protect, guide, and help. Second, calling God "our Father" means that specific fears should cease. To enter into a loving relationship with a loving Father through a loving Son eliminates any fear we could ever have of the wrath of God against our sin. Third, it brings an end to our hopelessness. There's no greater hope that children can have in a life wrecked by sin, shame, and despair than to be in the arms of a devoted, loving heavenly Father. It's also an end of loneliness. As our Father, God grants the church an intimacy and relationship with him that is all her own.

Is there anyone who knows all our failures and still loves us? Is there anyone who can give meaning to our hopeless lives? Is there anyone who can wipe away rolling tears? Our Father can.

Our Friend

Genuine friendship is more than action; it's devotion. When this devotion is the lens through which the church views God's company with us, that reality is so inexhaustible that it defies comprehension. God's benevolent offering of his beloved Son is most brightly on display in the Son's willingness to offer his life a ransom for his Father's friends: "Greater love has no one than this, that someone lay down his life for his friends" (John 15:13). And since the Father freely gave us his beloved Son, "how will he not also with him graciously give us all things?" (Rom. 8:32).

God holds his friends beautifully close to his heart from everlasting to everlasting. He doesn't abandon his church for a better, more faithful, or more loyal friend. He's never lamented choosing the church as his friend. When God established his friendship with the church, it had absolutely nothing to do with our faithfulness to him and everything to do with his faithfulness to us.

Through the millennia of the church's existence, her history often paints a disturbing picture of unfaithfulness, coldness, error, lethargy, and the like. But her friendship with God gives the church great comfort that though she may wander off the path at certain junctures, he always remains her faithful friend (Jer. 31:31–33; Heb. 8:8–10). There has never been a time in her patchy history, nor will there be a time in her future, when God will deny his friend, forsake his friend, or cast his friend aside.

God is both a Father and a friend to the church. These cherished relationships remind the church that God isn't remote and distant but is near and close. We are eternally bound to our Father and friend. He is uniquely ours, and we are uniquely his.

4

Our Savior and Head

Christ is the head of the church,
his body, and is himself its Savior.

EPHESIANS 5:23

TO GRASP CHRIST'S LOVE for his church is to plumb depths that have no bottom, find a treasure with no bounds, and climb heights that have no peak. All our redemption and salvation flows freely from that never-ending fountain of divine love. And such boundless love can only rightly be understood by visiting a bloody cross and an empty tomb.

Our Savior

The Greek word translated "Savior" means "one who preserves or rescues from natural dangers and afflictions." It carries the idea of deliverance from harm in order to preserve. A Savior is both a rescuer and protector. In his prophecy of the Messiah, Zechariah affirms that this anointed one will deliver us from the "hand of our enemies" (Luke 1:74). Who are our enemies, and why do we need rescuing? We need rescuing from our sin, God's wrath upon our sin, and death, which is a consequence of our sin (Isa. 59:2).

Jesus doesn't just excuse our sin and tell us to ignore its consequences. Christ and his bride are so intimately identified that they become united with one another in death and resurrection. Sinners come to the cross of Christ and receive, by faith, the wages of their sin—death. We don't die physically, but we die a required death through Christ, for he becomes our substitute and stands in our stead, taking upon himself the unmitigated wrath of his Father. What God requires of us because of our sin is paid in full by our beloved, the Lord Jesus Christ.

This beautiful union is so fixed and permanent that we are now taken into the eternal love that exists between the Father and the Son through the Spirit. The same love that flows unceasingly between the Father and the Son now directly flows to the bride.

Jesus is a worthy Savior not only because of his union with the nature and love of his Father but also because of union with the nature and love of his bride. He unites to her as she places her faith in him and thus he becomes the ground of her rescue and redemption. The bridegroom takes death upon himself and offers his meritorious work freely to his bride, that she may be welcomed into his family.

Our Head

The relationship between Christ and his bride is so multifaceted that merely one title will not satisfy all its beauty. Numerous rich metaphors throughout Scripture depict this divine exchange:

- Christ is both her founder and her foundation.
- Christ is both her Judge and her Savior.
- Christ is both her lover and her beloved.
- Christ is both her preserver and her hope.
- Christ is both her righteousness and her holiness.

However, perhaps no metaphorical phrase comes close to the gravity of Christ being the *head* of the church. Uniting himself to us in our nature not only makes Jesus a fit Savior for his bride but also makes him a fit head.

The phrase "head of the church" is not employed to identify Christ as the head of a company or the head of an organization. In Ephesians 5:23, Paul distinguishes Christ as "the head of the church, *his body*." The church isn't the result of human ingenuity. The living Christ is the head of a living organism.

Identifying Christ as the church's head denotes that he has sovereign lordship and supreme authority over her. As Jesus told his disciples when he commissioned them to evangelize the nations, "All authority in heaven and on earth has been given to me" (Matt. 28:18). The church doesn't belong to pastors or church members; the church belongs to Christ, and he is its sovereign head.

The church is intimately united to Christ as her Savior and head. This glorious truth will be the theme of the new song the bride will trumpet forth throughout the heavens:

> Worthy are you to take the scroll
>   and to open its seals,
> for you were slain, and by your blood you ransomed
>   people for God
>   from every tribe and language and people and nation.
>   (Rev. 5:9)

5

Our Helper and Beautifier

I will ask the Father, and he will
give you another Helper.

JOHN 14:6

ANY DISCUSSION ON THE CHURCH would be severely lacking without a close look at the presence and ministry of the Holy Spirit. Without him, the church would never have been founded. Godly leaders would never have been called, believers added, gifts distributed, service rendered, or growth realized.

Our Helper

To comfort the hearts of his despondent disciples, who have just learned that Jesus will soon be leaving them, he promises them a "Helper" (John 14:16). The word used in reference to the Holy Spirit means "one called to another's side, specifically to help and aid." It can also refer to an intercessor, an assistant, or one who pleads another's cause before a judge. The word itself reveals the all-encompassing role of the Spirit within the body of Christ. He is our Helper, Intercessor, Assistant, Advocate, Comforter, Counselor, and Sustainer.

What love Jesus has for the church! He doesn't leave her to fend for herself with her own devices, inventions, creativity, or wit. The Holy Spirit is sufficient to equip and empower you to discharge every aspect of the turning-the-world-upside-down ministry to which Jesus has called his church.

Our Beautifier

A chief work of the Spirit is to bring beauty out of chaos. In creation, the Spirit brought harmony out of formlessness and void (Gen. 1:2). In redemption, the Spirit brings life out of death and sin (John 3:5–6, 8). In sanctification, the Spirit brings beauty out of fallen flesh and wayward hearts (Rom. 8:9–11). The church becomes an instrument of Christ's beaming radiance in the world through the individual expressions of the work of grace by the Spirit in the lives of believers.

There's perhaps no better or more familiar expression of the Holy Spirit's beautifying work within the church than

Galatians 5:22–23, "The fruit of the Spirit is love, joy, peace, patience, kindness, goodness, faithfulness, gentleness, self-control."

At our salvation, the Spirit could instantaneously make us holy in action, word, and deed. However, he chooses instead to produce fruit in our lives to authenticate our union with Christ. Bearing fruit is a sign that we are *in* Christ, and he is *in* us.

Love. This is not the butterflies-in-the-stomach first-date kind of love or the tear-welling love at the reunion of friends. This is the sacrificial love that is conscious not of self-fulfillment but of self-giving. This kind of love is absolute in its resolve regardless of the response in return.

Joy. When the buds of joy blossom on the branch, the Spirit is generating more than mere happiness. The result is a joy unconditionally independent of the circumstances around us. The Spirit beautifies the church by anchoring her hope not in a kind of slap-happy giddiness so characteristic of worldly happiness, but in a joy founded on God himself.

Peace. This form of tranquil peace pillows our head amid the storms of life in the conscious assurance that our sovereign God is the controller of every infinitesimal detail and is working all things for our good and his ultimate glory (Rom. 8:28).

Patience. The Spirit beautifies the bride of Christ by producing within her self-restraint that doesn't retaliate. It never seeks revenge for wrongs done. It faces ever-arduous situations. It always endures.

Kindness. The Spirit desires to beautify the church by creating succulent fruit on the branch that yields the sweetness of our tender care for fellow believers and unbelievers alike, those inside the church and those outside

Goodness. This fruit conveys a determined resolve always to serve in the presence of God. In rejoicing, rebuke, exhortation, even in times of discipline, goodness toward wayward brothers and sisters keeps us beautifully demonstrating to every spectator that there are no perfect people—there is only a perfect Savior.

Faithfulness. Faithfulness is a work of the Holy Spirit (Acts 6:5). He beautifies the church through the fruit of faithfulness exhibited in her commitment and loyalty in serving others through Christ.

Gentleness. This fruit has been called "meekness" and speaks of a gentle blowing breeze that hints at strength but holds back in power. This isn't cowardice but is debased humility that keeps its power in check. Through the Spirit, the church can turn the world upside down through controlled humility.

Self-control. How utterly miserable we are at keeping our actions, minds, and hearts in check. How vitally necessary it is that the Holy Spirit grow this fruit upon the branches of our hearts. To be self-controlled is a command—a command to submit to the will of God at all times, in all circumstances, abandoning our selfish desires and sinful pleasures.

Christ sent the Holy Spirit to be both Helper and beautifier of the church. Fully deserving of our worship, the Spirit accomplishes a work in each believer, and thereby in the body of Christ, that should be recognized as tantamount to the works of both the Father and the Son.

6

A Pillar and Buttress of Truth

. . . a pillar and buttress of the truth.

1 TIMOTHY 3:15

WHAT CAN WE DO when the lies of this present age spring a leak in the church, which is supposed to hold back the torrent of the world's scheming deception? Some within the church would like to run for higher ground, cloistering themselves away from this growing danger. Others consider themselves impervious to the peril and rush to swim in the streams of the world, thinking they will never be polluted, only to end up drowning in the rushing waters of compromise. Still others, quite sincerely, just don't know how to respond.

Twisted Truth

Throughout the millennia since his fall, Satan has not altered his strategy of deceit. He has inundated every societal level with confusion and falsehood, from government, educational systems, mass media, and the family, to even the church. Paul warned the church at Corinth, "I am afraid that as the serpent deceived Eve by his cunning, your thoughts will be led astray from a sincere and pure devotion to Christ" (2 Cor. 11:3). Satan delights in leading the church away from faithful obedience to God and his word by inviting her members to swim and frolic in the waters of worldly lies. Unless we are held captive by God's word, the very heart of the church is susceptible to Satan's cunning deception. This is why, surrounded by a world of lies, the church must be ready to answer with God's truth.

Bearing Witness

Paul describes the church as the "pillar and buttress of the truth" (1 Tim. 3:15). That's a vivid way of saying that it's the church's task to *uphold* the truth. The Greek word for "buttress" means "support." This is the only time this word appears in the New Testament, and it defines the church as a bulwark of God's truth. The truth is her mission. The truth is her message. The truth is her reason for existing in the world.

In Paul's meticulous description, he is saying that once God's truth is removed from the church, her humanly devised structures, programs, and purpose for existing will collapse.

During the final moments of his life, standing before Pontius Pilate, Jesus declared that the reason he came into the world was to "bear witness to the truth." He added, "Everyone who is of the truth listens to my voice" (John 18:37). Notice in his stunning testimony that Jesus proclaimed that he came to bear witness to *the* truth—not a vague, obscure, nebulous, open-to-one's-own-interpretation kind of truth. Jesus came to bear witness to only one truth, God's truth, the only truth that exists. The only truth that will still be standing when heaven and earth pass away (Matt. 24:35).

Jesus is the full and definitive expression of God's absolute truth (Heb. 1:1–4). His whole ministry fulfilled the divine charge of truth-bearer. It was prophesied that Jesus would be "full of . . . truth" (John 1:14). He called himself "the truth" (John 14:6). The entirety of Jesus's teaching and preaching ministry was characterized as "the way of God truthfully" (Matt. 22:16).

All Scripture

The truth meant to be heralded by the church is found in a book. Paul identifies that book in 2 Timothy 3:16: "All Scripture is breathed out by God and profitable for teaching, for reproof, for correction, and for training in righteousness."

Paul doesn't say that the Bible is "breathed upon by God"; Scripture is "breathed out by God." God's word is God's breath. And this divine breath brings life to his church, molding and shaping us into the image of Christ, sanctifying and renewing our hearts, maturing our churches, and making them a gloriously beautiful place.

The truth given to us through Scripture is the pillar and buttress of the church, having the same authority, relevance, and sufficiency as God himself, for the Bible is his divine breath.

How does the church proclaim the truth of Christ in an ever-deeper cesspool of lies? First, she must separate herself and boldly refuse to be conformed to this present world—she must be continually transformed into imitators of Christ (Rom. 12:2; 1 Cor. 11:1). Second, the church must proclaim the countercultural truth of God's word, in love, before a hostile and unbelieving world (Col. 4:2–6). We must lovingly herald every command, commendation, and condemnation of Scripture. Third, the church must develop discerning wisdom, bringing every outside word captive to the obedience of Christ (2 Cor. 10:5). The world, full of hate, lies, deception, murder, half-truth, and even death, is illuminated by this light. So be what you are—pillars and buttresses of the truth in a world of lies.

In Spirit and Truth

*True worshipers will worship
the Father in spirit and truth.*

JOHN 4:23

THE APEX OF OUR FELLOWSHIP and communion with the triune God is holy worship. Worship of God originates with God, not man. Worship was never the idea or plan of man, as there's nothing in us that seeks after God or even desires to know him (Rom. 3:11). The desire to worship God is wrought in the heart of believers by the Holy Spirit. We love God because he first loved us. We seek God because he first sought us. We worship God because he commands such worship, and we willingly obey.

Beautiful Worship

John Owen said that the church should regularly be finding ways to express worship in manners that are "more decent, beautiful, and orderly."[1] What did Owen mean by "beautiful" worship? For worship to be biblically beautiful, Owen believed, it must focus on the triune God.

> All acceptable devotion in them that worship God is the effect of faith, which respects the precepts and promises of God alone. And the comeliness and beauty of gospel worship consisteth in its relation unto God by Jesus Christ, as the merciful high priest over his house, with the glorious administration of the Spirit therein.[2]

We would do well to keep in mind that "God is spirit, and those who worship him must worship in spirit and truth" (John 4:24). This is the only manner of devotion and worship that God accepts. God seeks those who will worship "in spirit." The text does not say "in *the* Spirit" but "in spirit." Jesus is not instructing believers to worship in the Holy Spirit but *with* or *in* the human spirit. He is telling the Samaritan woman in John 4 not only that he desires worship that flows from a knowledge of the truth of who he is, but also that he is looking for worshipers who will worship from the very depth of their inner being—their spirit.

Authentic biblical worship occurs only when the very core of our being is employed in worshiping God. Our lips may mouth the words, our hands may be lifted upward, our eyes may fill with tears, but unless these expressions flow from "the effect of faith," as Owen describes, our worship is mere performance. Valid worship proceeds from the heart of faith, for "without faith it is impossible to please him, for whoever would draw near to God must believe that he exists and that he rewards those who seek him" (Heb. 11:6). Worship isn't born in the void of our conscience but proceeds from truth. The truth of who God is as revealed in his word, the understanding of who Christ is and what he accomplished in his incarnation, the realization of who the Spirit is and what he is currently doing in our lives. Without truth born in faith, worship becomes ordinary, humdrum, and even carnal.

Gospel Simplicity

Gospel-shaped worship is beautiful when it flows from a mind informed by truth and a heart willing to abandon all for the sake of communion with God. The gospel simplicity that replaces ceremonialist performance is the message of salvation through faith in God's final Word to man—Jesus Christ. He is infinitely more beautiful than gold or jewels. Christ's sacrificial death on the cross has obtained "an eternal redemption" for his people

(Heb. 9:12), making him "the mediator of a new covenant" (Heb. 9:15). Before, there was trepidation; now there is boldness. Before, there was slavery; now there is liberty. Before, there was complexity; now there is simplicity.

Worshipers are now free to come before the throne of grace, bypassing the folderol of the old way, now having access to a better way, for we "are no longer strangers and aliens, but you are now fellow citizens with the saints and members of the household of God" (Eph. 2:18–19).

The beauty of gospel worship, the worship with which we must concern ourselves as the bride of Christ, is found not in ritual and ceremony but in Christ and Christ alone. There is no glory in any other worship than the worship that comes by and is exclusively in Jesus Christ. For in him, the beauty of worship consists and becomes simple, spiritual, and heavenly.

8

Shepherding the Flock

Shepherd the flock of God that is among you.

I PETER 5:2

FAITHFUL LEADERS BEAUTIFY THE CHURCH when they recognize that they are mere representatives of Christ and subordinate to him in all things. In other words, any authority these governing servants possess is a delegated authority from their sovereign head. When Jesus commissioned and sent out his disciples, he said, "All authority in heaven and on earth has been given to *me*. . . . And behold, *I am* with you always, to the end of the age" (Matt. 28:18, 20). Any authority leaders within the church retain is Christ's authority. That vicarious authority promises that he will be with us, working in and through us to exercise such jurisdiction in the love and care of his bride.

When leaders within the church admit and demonstrate that they are subservient to Christ, all other ministries within the church display a rare beauty that shines with the glory of Christ. In short, the church isn't a man-centered, egotistical spectacle but is a Christ-exalting organism led by gospel-driven servanthood. All who desire to make the church beautiful adopt as their life motto "Not from men nor through man, but through Jesus Christ" (Gal. 1:1).

The Ministry of a Pastor

Scripture is clear that the primary position of leadership and care within the body of Christ is the position of pastor. This office is known by many titles used interchangeably throughout the New Testament, such as *elder*, *bishop* or *overseer*, *shepherd* or *pastor*, *preacher*, and *teacher*.

It's evident that a pastor's role is singularly bound up with the varied duties of elder, overseer, shepherd, preacher, and teacher, all of which serve to care for, guide, instruct, and watch over the flock of God. To serve in this role or office, one must meet a high standard. Each man of God needs to endure a time of testing or proving to be placed in such a lofty position of shepherding oversight (1 Tim. 3:2–3).

A church radiates the beauty of Christ only when they are faithful to appoint men who themselves are beautiful in character and holiness. We all have heard and read devastating stories of churches that lose all credibility and destroy their witness because they appoint men to leadership positions who fail to meet those qualifications. That is not to say that churches must find perfect men to serve. There are no sinless leaders. Instead, the church needs to find men who, through proper testing and refining, demonstrate that they meet the biblical injunction and qualifications to serve.

To be a biblically faithful pastor and faithfully beautify the church, one's heart must beat in rhythm with the heart of Christ, both privately and publicly. There is no room for error in doctrine or failure in holiness.

The Ministry of a Deacon

In addition to the office of pastor another critical role within the life of the body is that of a deacon. While Scripture doesn't specifically detail a deacon's responsibilities within the church, it does emphasize the key qualification for such an office—moral character. The attention Scripture devotes to the moral integrity, spiritual maturity, and doctrinal purity of those who serve the body of Christ highlights the importance of holiness within the life of the church and how such holiness serves to beautify.

A deacon is a servant. Originally, the verb *diakoneō* may have meant "serve tables" (Acts 6:2). But more broadly, the noun *diakonos* came to represent those who give themselves to any service to meet the needs of the people. A deacon is, like the governing authorities, a "servant for your good" and a "servant of God" (Rom. 13:3–4).

If we were to sum up a deacon's qualifications in a single phrase, it would be "full of the Spirit" (Acts 6:3; cf. Eph. 5:18). A deacon's moral character must be above reproach in all things. In public, deacons must prove exemplary in life, speech, integrity, and heart. In private, deacons must also evidence commitment to the truth of God's word and the holiness of their homes.

A deacon beautifies the church, first, by being a visible, unassuming, unadorned representative of the Lord Jesus Christ. Second, the deacon is a selfless servant to all. He doesn't pick and choose his favorite people to help. He willingly and sacrificially sets his desires aside to serve the widow, the hungry, the poor, the grieving, the helpless, and the sick alike. Third, the deacon helps "bring justice to the fatherless" and pleads "the widow's cause" (Isa. 1:17). He helps beautify the church by caring for those who have no one else to care for them.

Christ, the supreme head of the church, doesn't leave us to grope about in darkness, trying to discover innovative ways to lead and help ourselves. He's dispensed all we need and administers his bride's authority, leadership, and care by assigning specific biblical offices to be his representatives on earth.

9

Feeding the Flock

Preach the word.

2 TIMOTHY 4:2

IN 2 TIMOTHY 4, with sweeping brushstrokes, Paul paints a beautiful picture of an undershepherd.

Pastoral Charge

After a series of exhortations to Timothy, Paul begins one final injunction by imploring Timothy, "I charge you . . ." (2 Tim. 4:1). In Greek, this phrase is not composed of three words like our English translation but is one strong word that expresses an earnest testimony, solemn command, and strong urging. Paul isn't offering suggestions here but is voicing a strong compulsion for fervent ministry faithfulness. He, in effect, escorts Timothy into an ancient courtroom and says, "The full case of the entirety of your ministry, Timothy, will be drawn up against you in the court of God, where Christ Jesus is the Judge."

This is a summons for every man of God who has been called to the lofty yet humbling task of proclaiming the unsearchable riches of Christ—to stand in the eternal courtroom of God's presence. The pastor will not have a team of lawyers to argue his case or witnesses to testify of his good works. Still, the whole of his ministry—every sermon preached, every prayer prayed, every deed performed—will be open before the examining, flaming eyes of Christ (Rev. 19:12).

This isn't meant to frighten those contemplating a call to ministry, or seminarians preparing to enter the church, or even those who have been fulfilling their pastoral charge for decades. This charge reminds us of the seriousness with which we must view the calling of being the representatives of Christ in the world. Ministry isn't a quick way to make a buck. The church isn't a fast track to renown or notoriety.

God elevates the call to serve the church to a level of eternal scrutiny, warning us to think twice before beginning the journey: "Not many of you should become teachers, my brothers, for you know that we who teach will be judged with greater strictness" (James 3:1). All ministry is to be carried out with constant mindfulness that everything we do is under the watchful eye of God. Therefore, no argument is sustainable for a lackadaisical attitude of wasting time on frivolous things at the expense of tending the flock of God.

"Preach the Word"

Paul distills the pastor's paramount task to a single phrase: "Preach the word" (2 Tim. 4:2). Such a simple statement, yet the pulse of every undershepherd of Christ. A preacher is to herald the word! The word translated "preach" is the Greek verb meaning "herald, proclaim, and announce publicly." During the Roman Empire, the word was often associated with those sent from the emperor's imperial court to publicly deliver a message to the people.

What is it we herald?

Paul designates the object of our message as "the word" (2 Tim. 4:2). That is, "all Scripture" (2 Tim. 3:16). Paul's sermons were not filled with intellectual platitudes of man's seeming superior wisdom. He wrote, "I, when I came to you, brothers, did not come proclaiming to you the testimony of God with lofty speech or wisdom" (1 Cor. 2:1). Lest anyone think gospel heralds have a message of mere interpretive opinion or suggestion, we're reminded that "what we proclaim is not ourselves, but Jesus Christ as Lord" (2 Cor. 4:5). Nothing should stand as a dam between the refreshing truth of God and the arid lands of the human heart. Only the unceasing proclamation of Christ is sufficient to quench such longing thirst.

How often are we to proclaim the word? "In season and out of season" (2 Tim. 4:2).

Pastors are to broadcast every jot and tittle of God's word when the message is *in* and when the message is *out*. When those around you are interested and when they aren't interested. When the message is popular and when it's not popular. The whims of the people must never determine the frequency and substance of preaching. Regardless of the popularity of the message, the pastor is to be ready "in season and out of season" to "reprove, rebuke, and exhort" (2 Tim. 4:2). As with a military guard or a watchman on a tower warning of impending danger to the city, there's no off-season for the pastor. There is only absolute fearlessness.

Feeding the flock of God is a fundamental duty in contributing to the beauty and loveliness of the church. As God's truth is proclaimed, men and women are saved and sanctified, and the church is made beautiful.

10

Good News

How beautiful upon the mountains
are the feet of him who brings good news.

THE NEW TESTAMENT is unmistakably clear that God has called his church to be the principal agency for heralding the gospel of Christ. The believers in the church of Acts were zealous and passionate proclaimers of the good news of Jesus Christ. Peter's enemies told him and the other apostles, "You have filled Jerusalem with your teaching" (Acts 5:28). In response to their evangelistic efforts, Paul and his fellow missionaries were accused of turning the world upside down (Acts 17:6). As a result, "the Lord added to their number day by day those who were being saved" (Acts 2:47).

The Gospel of God

Paul's introduction to his letter to the church in Rome makes it quite apparent that the entire epistle's theme is the good news of "the gospel of God" (Rom. 1:1). This good news of the gospel is

- "the good news of the kingdom of God" (Luke 16:16),
- "good news . . . of Jesus Christ" (Acts 8:12),
- "good news of peace" (Acts 10:36),
- "the gospel of the grace of God" (Acts 20:24),
- "the gospel of his Son" (Rom. 1:9),
- "the gospel of your salvation" (Eph. 1:13),
- "the gospel of the glory of the blessed God" (1 Tim. 1:11).

Surrounded by *bad* news at every turn, the church has been entrusted with *good* news, the good news of the gospel, which finds its foundation in God himself. The gospel is not an earthly message but a heavenly message. Paul says that this is the "gospel *of God*" (Rom. 1:1). The gospel is *about* God—his holiness, love, grace, wrath, and righteousness. But Paul's main emphasis here is that the gospel is *from* God. He is the single author and architect of the gospel. The gospel doesn't originate in the church. The church didn't invent the gospel. The gospel is a message given to the bride of Christ announcing his mediatorial triumph over sin, death, and the world.

The word translated "gospel" is a compound in Greek, *euangelion*. The prefix *eu* means "good." The primary root word *angelion* means "messenger" or "message." When those two words are placed together, the word *gospel* simply means "good news." The gospel is the good news of salvation through God's Son, Jesus Christ.

What is the message of God's beautiful gospel?

God sent his Son, the second person of the Trinity, the Lord Jesus Christ, to rescue sinners. He was born of a virgin and lived a sinlessly perfect and obedient life under the law. He was crucified on a cross as a substitute to pay the penalty of God's wrath against the sins of all those who would ever believe. In his body, he bore on that tree the punishment due to sinners and his perfect righteousness was imputed to them, making them acceptable in the sight of God. He was buried in a borrowed tomb and on the third day rose from the dead. He ascended back to the authority and power of the right hand of his Father to intercede for all believers. Now, everyone who by faith "calls on the name of the Lord will be saved" (Rom. 10:13). This isn't only good news; it's beautifully good news.

No church has the freedom to tamper with, tweak, add to, or subtract from the good news of Jesus Christ—we are just to herald it. For there is nothing more beautiful and lovely in the sight of God than the extricating of sinners from the kingdom of darkness and delivering them to the kingdom of light.

Gospel Zeal

The impetus for our gospel zeal is the promise that

> all the ends of the earth shall see
> the salvation of our God. (Isa. 52:10)

All evangelistic and missionary endeavors are fueled by the confidence that Christ is enthroned as the head of the church and has promised to ransom men and women from "every tribe and language and people and nation" (Rev. 5:8–9). This assurance fueled John Calvin to write to the king when evangelistic efforts were harshly suppressed in his homeland of France:

> Indeed, we are quite aware of what . . . lowly little men we are. . . . But our doctrine must tower unvanquished above all the glory and above all the might of the world, for it is not of us, but of the living God and his Christ whom the Father has appointed to "rule from sea to sea, and from the rivers even to the ends of the earth" (Ps. 72:8).[1]

"It is not of us," Calvin wrote. There's such a God-centeredness to the gospel that we cannot claim it as our own. It didn't originate with the church, for we merely "have this treasure in jars of clay, to show that the surpassing power belongs to God and not to us" (2 Cor. 4:7). The gospel is God's gospel, and we are called to proclaim it with all our might.

11

In Remembrance

Do this in remembrance of me.
1 CORINTHIANS 11:24

THE ORDINANCES OF BAPTISM and the Lord's Supper are two specific ways in which God accomplishes his beautifying work within his church. Some traditions call these two mandates sacraments to denote that they are *holy* things and should therefore be kept holy by the church. Regardless of what they are labeled, these two ordinances are taught in Scripture and are reserved by God to be practiced exclusively by the church.

Baptism

Baptism is an act of obedience in a new life of faith and is not a suggested practice but a clear command, for discipleship is not complete without baptism.

Baptism is beautifully associated with repentance and faith. In Matthew 3, multitudes come to John the Baptist to be baptized as a symbol of their repentance from sin and turning to God (Matt. 3:6). Baptism is a symbol that points to saving faith; it is not the conveyer of saving grace (Eph. 2:8–9). Biblical baptism signifies a turning away from sin, a full-fledged embrace of Christ, and a believer's willingness to identify with him in his death, burial, and resurrection so that we can now "walk in newness of life" (Rom. 6:4).

Baptism beautifies the church in several ways. First, it exalts Christ by being a visible expression and reminder of his death, burial, and resurrection. Second, it energizes onlookers to obey Christ by making their own public confession of faith. Third, baptism announces the gospel. Apart from the gospel's proclamation in preaching, baptism is the most visual portrayal of the gospel possessed by the church. Fourth, baptism serves as a sign and a warning—a sign that forgiveness is available to all who place their faith in Christ, and a warning that unless you repent, "you will all likewise perish" (Luke 13:3).

As God's gift to his church, baptism is how he incorporates us into his fold, strengthens his body, beautifies his church, and draws more to himself.

The Lord's Supper

Paul recalls the meal the Lord Jesus celebrated with his disciples the night before his death (Luke 22:14–23; 1 Cor. 11:23–26). Originally the meal of Passover, this old covenant feast was transformed by Jesus into a meal of infinitely greater significance. Rather than looking back to deliverance from Egypt, the Lord's Supper causes believers to reflect back to when their sins were atoned for by God's spotless Lamb while also looking forward to the great marriage supper of the Lamb, when we shall bask together in the resplendent glory of our Father.

The simple symbolic elements of bread and the cup—Christ's flesh and blood—become a beautifying influence upon the church as the supper demonstrates our remembering, loving, and examining.

Remembering. The supper becomes a path to congregational beauty as we come together to remember Christ. We need look no further than to the Lord's Supper to see Jesus, for through this celebratory meal, he has left us a portrait of himself to remember him. The very elements point to Christ. Without diving into the varied views, we may say that the bread represents his incarnate sinless flesh nailed to the cross, and the cup signifies the blood that poured forth for the atonement of sin. When eaten and drunk amid corporate worship, these elements together become one of the most explicit pictures of Jesus that the church retains.

Loving. The very symbols present within the meal highlight the selfless, sacrificial love poured forth by Christ on the cross. The Lord's Table is one of the foremost places within the church to gather in mutual love and reconciliation. This is why the Lord's Supper is not to be celebrated alone, for it is a congregational meal to demonstrate and foster genuine love among the people of God. At the table, we're reminded that the church is one, and our mutual love radiates forth to display a beautiful bride before a watching world.

Examining. For this type of mutual love and reconciliation to be present, each of us must examine himself or herself (1 Cor. 11:27–28). By examining ourselves, we perform a mental and internal survey of our relationship with Christ, our relationships with others, and our private and public sins. Now, the Lord's Supper isn't for the sinless—for no one is without sin—but is for those who have thoroughly examined every aspect of their lives, so far as is possible, and confessed and repented of sin with a wholehearted desire to walk with Christ.

While baptism identifies us with the death, burial, and resurrection of our Lord and the testimony of faith wrought within our hearts, the Lord's Supper is the frequent reminder that believers must remember the Lord, love one another, and continually deal with their sin. In these ways, both baptism and the Lord's Supper are visible ordinances whereby the Holy Spirit sanctifies believers. Through our participation in both, the Lord has provided a way in which his bride is inseparably linked to his cross and resurrection as the ultimate glory of her beauty.

12

Walking Worthy

Walk in a manner worthy of the calling
to which you have been called.

EPHESIANS 4:1

PAUL SPENDS THE FIRST three chapters of his letter to the Ephesian church assembling a doctrinal framework upon which he will hang principles of right behavior. Paul never offers the *how* without first giving us the *why*. These first three chapters of Ephesians are the *why*—who we are in Christ. Paul then shifts his discussion in chapter 4 to how believers are to live.

"I therefore" (v. 1) is an intentional shift from the theological to the practical—*how* God's people should live as a result of *who* they are. This whole applicatory section of Ephesians 4:1–6:20

is built upon the firm bedrock of Christ as the cornerstone of his church and the Spirit who empowers such living (Eph. 3:16).

Walking in Christ

"I . . . urge you to walk" (Eph. 4:1). The metaphor of *walking* appears throughout Paul's letters and is always connected with an urgency in the Christian life. Paul understands this urgency. The admonitions Paul offers are dispensed not as suggestions or good ideas but as unequivocal commands for faithfulness in *being* and *living as* the body of Christ. This is your obedience in the gospel—you who once *walked* in transgressions and sins (Eph. 2:1–2)—you now must *walk* in the good works God has intended for you (Eph. 2:10).

Throughout the New Testament, the verb "walk" is a present tense Greek word referring to a continuous mode of conduct. The infinitive "to walk" can be rendered "to live." In his instructions to the church, Paul uses "walk" in this way to guarantee that they comprehend what correct Christian living is and what it is not. For Paul, "walking" is shorthand for practical Christian living—living out what has been planted within.

Other New Testament writers also employ the same image of walking to define the life of a believer. For instance, John says Christians are not to "walk in darkness" (1 John 1:6; 2:11). Believers should not continue to live in the sin from which they were rescued. In his Gospel record, John taught that Jesus was the true light for a sin-darkened world (John 1:4–5), and no one can rightly claim to be a true believer and follower of Christ who continues to walk in sinful darkness.

Walking in the Light

In contrast to the darkness of the world, the bride of Christ is to "walk in the light" (1 John 1:7). Those who walk in the light do so because the Spirit of God has regenerated them and given them new life in Christ. When church members' feet are firmly fixed on the path of light, their lives will reflect the glory and majesty of the one who is the light. Your daily actions, attitudes, conversations, thoughts, and works will reflect a light-filled Christlikeness. Walking in the light results in a godly attitude so that, instead of lashing out at difficult people or becoming angry with those who disagree, you're actually brought into "fellowship with one another" (1 John 1:7).

As a result of walking in the light, the body of Christ also walks by the Spirit and therefore walks "worthy." At the precise moment of someone's salvation, the Holy Spirit begins to live within that person. Puritan Richard Sibbes believed that at the exact instant the Spirit takes up residence within us, he begins to knit our hearts to God and Jesus Christ. Sibbes explained, "The Spirit is the bond of union between Christ and us, and between God and us."[1] The role of the Spirit is to intimately acquaint us with the Father and the Son. He establishes communion between us and empowers us to walk. When the Spirit is present, he transforms our lives from one degree of glory to another. As he molds us into the image of Christ, the Spirit collectively empowers the church to walk in a Christlike manner.

While it is the Spirit who unleashes the dynamic power to walk in the Christian life, it is the individual Christian who must put one foot in front of the other. The Spirit fills every true believer within the household of faith, but those individual believers must work, teach, pray, and worship, propelling the church into a closer walk and joy in Jesus. The Spirit doesn't work for us, preach for us, evangelize for us, or even worship for us. He empowers his people to do all these things, but it is their responsibility to walk.

A church that is beautiful in the eyes of her bridegroom is a church that is walking "in a manner worthy of the calling to which you have been called" (Eph. 4:1). It is living lives that regularly confess sin and preeminently desire to walk according to the Spirit and not according to the flesh. Living lives that reflect their Master and image him forth to a watching world. Living lives that yearn to know him and have his gospel power flow in them for his good pleasure. Living lives that mutually display to all who see that the church is genuinely walking worthy.

Blessed Persecution

All who desire to live a godly life in
Christ Jesus will be persecuted.

2 TIMOTHY 3:12

IN FOXE'S BOOK OF MARTYRS, we read the account of Protestant Reformer John Hooper, who was arrested and imprisoned when Mary I (eventually known as Bloody Mary) ascended the throne and immediately began to usher England back to Roman Catholicism. On numerous occasions, Hooper was ushered before assembled councils and commanded to recant his "Protestant heresy." Every time, he refused.

On February 9, 1555, Bishop Hooper was led to his place of execution in Gloucester, tied to a stake, and burned. When he reached the erected place of his death, an iron hoop was placed around his chest to secure him to the wooden stake. As the kindling was placed around him, he caught two bundles in his hands, kissed them, and put them under his arms. On that cold morning the blustery English wind was so fierce that the flames barely touched him. The bottom half of his body began to burn, but only slightly, while the fire never reached his upper body, except his hair. Hopper cried: "Lord Jesus, have mercy upon me! Lord Jesus, have mercy upon me! Lord Jesus, receive my spirit!" These were his final words that emerged from the flames. Little by little he burned. First one finger, then the next. One arm fell off into the fire, and then the next, until finally he yielded up his spirit.

Paul warned Timothy, "All who desire to live a godly life in Christ Jesus will be persecuted" (2 Tim. 3:12). Paul was deeply persuaded that conflict is inevitable between the church composed of those living righteously and those in the world who revel in their ungodliness. There is an undeniable tension between light and darkness.

Lest we think the church is immune to or exempt from persecutions and sufferings in our modern age, Jesus reminds us, "The world hates you" (John 15:18).

Reasons for Persecution

In the conclusion of his Beatitude statements in Matthew 5, Jesus pronounces a divine blessing upon those who suffer persecution.[1] Why will his hearers face persecution? Because they exhibit the godly characteristics of the previous beatitudes. Jesus defines persecution and suffering arising from two sources.

First, true disciples of Christ are persecuted "for righteousness" (Matt. 5:10). The type of righteousness on display in the beatitudes—humility, meekness, peacemaking, hunger for righteousness—will inevitably elicit persecution from the world. The ungodly witness the church's righteousness and see such holiness as a condemnation of their unrighteous behavior. In response, they lash out in ridicule and malign the church through severe forms of persecution and suffering.

Second, true disciples of Christ are persecuted "on my [Jesus's] account," or as several translations put it, "because of me [Jesus]" (Matt. 5:11). He highlights a particular *name*— a Christological title—that, when we are identified with it, causes persecution and ridicule. According to Luke 6:22, many will instigate particular hostility against unbelievers "on account of the Son of Man." This specific title identifies Jesus as a King of divine, heavenly origin, who will reign over a universal and eternal kingdom and is worthy of worship by all peoples of the earth. When the church identifies with the Christ of the Bible—divine ruler of the cosmos, worthy of all worship—she exhibits an alien righteousness that is unique in character. This righteousness is not of her own making or invention. This distinctive, heavenly righteousness has been gifted to her by Christ on the cross, who desired to beautify his bride by granting her an unparalleled message: Jesus is King.

Expressions of Persecution

Jesus says in Matthew 5:11 that others will "revile you." Reviling is the picture of someone mocking and verbally shaming you, pronouncing over you humiliating and discrediting words.

Second, the word "persecute" in verse 11 means "run after, pursue, or run out." Jesus is warning his disciples that they may be sought from town to town by those driven by evil intentions, may endure violent abuse, and may even be turned over to the authorities.

Third, verse 11 states that adversaries will "utter all kinds of evil against you falsely on my account." The persecutors of Jesus's followers will raise allegations against them that have no basis in reality but are lies.

There is no substance to deceitful lies, false accusations, and mockery invented to persecute those within the church. A church devoted to righteousness, godliness, and the gospel of Christ will be persecuted and reviled because that same righteousness, godliness, and gospel come as an indictment against the sinful lifestyle of unbelievers.

Rejoice and Be Glad!

If we were only given Matthew 5:11, we might despair. But Jesus gives us more: "Rejoice and be glad, for your reward is great in heaven, for so they persecuted the prophets who were before you" (Matt. 5:12). Rejoice while suffering? Be glad amid ridicule? How can this be? This mystery is unveiled in the depth of our unyielding assurance that being with Jesus in glory will far more than reward us for any suffering we have faced in this life.

To "be glad" is to enjoy a state of utter happiness and well-being. "Rejoice" is similar in meaning to being glad but is more intense. This denotes extreme gladness and extreme joy.

The forward-looking faith of Moses is an example to us all: "He considered the reproach of Christ greater wealth than the treasures of Egypt, for he was looking to the reward" (Heb. 11:26).

14

We Are One

There is one body.

EPHESIANS 4:4

ONENESS AMONG THE PEOPLE of God is a defining characteristic of the church. We don't have to read far into the New Testament until we find Jesus speaking of the oneness of his bride. The content of his high priestly prayer in John 17 abounds with oneness petitions. Without this unity, the world is likely to see the church as a human organization devised by creative ingenuity, not a body of divine origin. Discord plagues man-made institutions—love, peace, harmony, community, and fellowship eventually break down. Jesus is praying that when the world views the church, it will see not a man-made organization but a divine organism born from God. The church's growing *oneness* is what defines the church as having an *otherness*.

Since unity of the faith is indispensable to the church's ministries, her knowledge of Christ, her maturity in the faith, and her imaging of God to the world, we must consider it a command and duty to preserve and perfect this unity within the church. What are some practical ways individual believers can foster a true unity that manifests itself within the one body?

Unity Requires One-Anothering

There are fifty-nine "one another" statements in the New Testament that speak directly to what we are to do and how we are to act toward each other. For example:

- "Be at peace with one another" (Mark 9:50).
- "Love one another" (John 13:34).
- "Serve one another" (Gal. 5:13).
- "Forgiving one another" (Eph. 4:32).
- "Admonishing one another" (Col. 3:16).
- "Encourage one another" (1 Thess. 4:18).
- "Do not speak evil against one another" (James 4:11).
- "Show hospitality to one another" (1 Pet. 4:9).

As these samples show, the "one another" statements divert attention from ourselves to others. Others become the focus of our ministry.

The "one another" passages are not suggestions for a successful life but commands for right Christian living. Unity is impossible when we consider ourselves more significant than others. The anthem of disunity is "me, myself, and I." We desire our opinions to be heard, our views considered, and our plans fulfilled. We could go as far as to say that unity requires the obliteration of self. It is the complete denial of self to maintain love, fellowship, and peace within the church. By obeying these injunctions, believers ultimately obey the second great commandment, to love one's neighbor as oneself (Mark 12:31), which puts the gospel of Christ on display as the transformative power it claims to possess. Have you wondered how you can beautify the bride of Christ? "One another" fellow believers.

Unity Requires Sanctified Truthfulness

True unity in the church exists only where her members declare with one harmonious voice, "Your word is truth" (John 17:17). Based on the inerrant and sufficient word of God, sound doctrine is essential in fostering true unity. In John 17, Jesus prays that his people would be sanctified in the truth (v. 17). "Sanctify" means "make holy." It involves setting something or someone apart from sin. Jesus says that God's word contains the proper ingredients for holiness: "Your word is truth." Therefore, since Scripture is the means whereby believers are made holy, our churches mustn't be a smorgasbord of varied beliefs and ideas, but must be an exquisitely set table offering the scriptural nourishment that causes growth into the image of Christ. If a church is seemingly unified without sound theology, her unity resides in amusing sentimentality or overt falsehood. True unity consists of sanctified truthfulness that bases every ministry, sermon, and decision upon the word of God.

Unity Requires Gospel Fidelity

As we have already explored, any church that doesn't have a biblical understanding of the gospel cannot be called a true church. The key here is not only the gospel in the evangelistic terms of justifying, forgiving, and saving, but also the gospel in terms of sanctifying, growing, and maturing as Christians. Unity within the church is a wholehearted commitment to gospel fidelity within her people's everyday lives. From how we teach children to how we train for ministry, we must be committed to the faithfulness, dependability, and transformative effects of the gospel to have lasting results. The gospel unifies the very culture of the church. If for one moment we imagine that our creativity, entrepreneurship, initiative, or even intellect is the impetus by which Christians grow in Christ, we will be fractured. Authentic unity is fostered by a daily awareness of our need for the life, death, burial, resurrection, and ascension of Jesus.

———

Unity is critical because it fosters maturity, doctrinal stability, discernment, a loving vocabulary, Christlike growth, church-wide equipping, and spiritual building. Our oneness reflects Christ, who beams forth his glory in every sphere of the church to make her increasingly beautiful. May our prayer echo the words of Charles Spurgeon: "Bless this our beloved church: keep them still in unity and earnestness of heart. In all fresh advances that we hope to make, be with us and help us."[1]

Epilogue

The king has brought me into his chambers.

SONG OF SOLOMON 1:4

A KING'S INNER CHAMBERS are the most secluded, private, and heavily guarded rooms within his palace. Here, his bride is welcomed as his peculiar treasure and joy.

This book has essentially served as a visit to the sacred chambers where Christ dwells alone with his church. We have been led into the inner workings of the triune God as he rescues and sanctifies a people and makes them fit for his glory. Here, we are called his friends, his bride, his possession, his children, his house. Here, we can call him our Father, our Friend, our Savior, our Head, our Helper, and our Beautifier. Within these chambers, the church is robed in beauty, arrayed in loveliness, and set upon a path of lifelong adoration, intimate fellowship, selfless service, and gospel proclamation.

The church isn't just about organization, leadership, function, and vision. There's something much more beautiful and lovely to recognize. The church is about people being rescued, redeemed, and renewed. The church is about savoring, rejoicing, and service. The church is about proclaiming, enduring, and walking. The church is about *being* the bride adorned, beautiful, and lovely.

Though we visit these chambers often, one day our king will invite us into his chambers forever. That celebration will be inaugurated with the marriage supper of the Lamb. On this day, the bridegroom will consummate all things, and we shall be arrayed in garments white as snow as we enter eternal, unbroken fellowship with the Father, Son, and Holy Spirit.

This book was meant for people who find themselves in a million different places, scattered abroad in local churches in every continent of the world, faithfully plodding, praying for a renewed hope and glimpse of the beauty and loveliness of the church.

The King has thrown open the doors.

He welcomes you to enter.

He bids you to gaze upon his bride and proclaim, "Behold, you are beautiful!" (Song 1:15).

Notes

Introduction

1. Jonathan Edwards, "The Church's Marriage to Her Sons, and to Her God," in *Sermons and Discourses, 1743–1758*, ed. Wilson H. Kimnach, vol. 25 of *The Works of Jonathan Edwards* (New Haven, CT: Yale University Press, 2006), 187.

2. Jonathan Edwards, *Writings on the Trinity, Grace, and Faith*, ed. Sang Hyun Lee, vol. 21 of *The Works of Jonathan Edwards* (New Haven, CT: Yale University Press, 2003), 142.

Chapter 1: You Are Beautiful

1. John Gill, *An Exposition of the Book of Solomon's Song* (London: William Hill Collingridge, 1854), 57.

2. Jonathan Edwards, "Miscellanies," 271, in *The Miscellanies, Entry Nos. a–z, aa–zz, 1–500*, ed. Thomas A. Schafer, vol. 13 of *The Works of Jonathan Edwards* (New Haven, CT: Yale University Press, 1994), 374.

Chapter 2: The Household of God

1. John Owen, *The Works of John Owen*, ed. William H. Goold, 24 vols. (1850–1855; repr., vols. 1–16, Edinburgh: Banner of Truth,

1965–1968), 1:485. See also Sinclair Ferguson, *John Owen on the Christian Life* (Edinburgh: Banner of Truth, 1987), 158.

2. Ferguson, *John Owen*, 159.

Chapter 7: In Spirit and Truth

1. John Owen, *Brief Instruction*, in *The Works of John Owen*, ed. William H. Goold, 24 vols. (1850–1855; repr., vols. 1–16, Edinburgh: Banner of Truth, 1965–1968), 15:467. See Joel R. Beeke and Mark Jones, "John Owen on the Christian Sabbath and Worship," chap. 41 in *A Puritan Theology* (Grand Rapids, MI: Reformation Heritage, 2012), 653–79.

2. Owen, *Works*, 15:467.

Chapter 10: Good News

1. John Calvin, prefatory address to King Francis, in *Institutes of the Christian Religion*, ed. John T. McNeill, trans. Ford Lewis Battles (Philadelphia: Westminster Press, 1960), 13.

Chapter 12: Walking Worthy

1. Richard Sibbes, "A Description of Christ," in *The Complete Works of Richard Sibbes*, ed. Alexander B. Grosart, 7 vols. (1862–1864; repr., Edinburgh: Banner of Truth, 1978–1983), 1:17.

Chapter 13: Blessed Persecution

1. This chapter, particularly this section and the following, draws upon Dustin Benge, "The Persecution Driven Life," *reformation21*, August 31, 2018, https://www.reformation21.org/blogs/the-persecution -driven-life.php.

Chapter 14: We Are One

1. Charles H. Spurgeon, *The Pastor in Prayer* (London: Elliot Stock, 1893), 143.

Scripture Index

Union

We fuel reformation in churches and lives.

Union Publishing invests in the next generation of leaders with theology that gives them a taste for a deeper knowledge of God. From books to our free online content, we are committed to producing excellent resources that will refresh, transform, and grow believers and their churches.

We want people everywhere to know, love, and enjoy God, glorifying him in everything they do. For this reason, we've collected hundreds of free articles, podcasts, book chapters, and video content for our free online collection. We also produce a fresh stream of written, audio, and video resources to help you to be more fully alive in the truth, goodness, and beauty of Jesus.

If you are hungry for reformational resources that will help you delight in God and grow in Christ, we'd love for you to visit us at unionpublishing.org.

unionpublishing.org

Union Series

  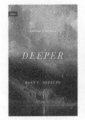

Full & Concise Editions

Rejoice and Tremble | What Does It Mean to Fear the Lord?

Deeper | How Does God Change Us?

The Loveliest Place | Why Should We Love the Local Church?

The Union series invites readers to experience deeper enjoyment of God through four interconnected values: delighting in God, growing in Christ, serving the church, and blessing the world.

For more information, visit **crossway.org**.